Unconditional Eternal Security Is It Scriptural?

Steven Waldron

Copyright 2022 by Steven Waldron.

Published 2022.

Printed in the United States of America.

All rights reserved.

No portion of this book may be reproduced, stored in a retrieval system, or transmitted in any form or by any means – electronic, mechanical, photocopy, recording, scanning, or other – except for brief quotations in critical reviews or articles, without the prior written permission of the author.

ISBN 978-1-950647-76-7

Cover image: CanStockPhoto by kwest19

Publishing assistance by BookCrafters, Parker, Colorado.
www.bookcrafters.net

Acknowledgements

Jan and Joe at BookCrafters are absolutely amazing, and a joy to work with. Their kindness and patience to someone like me, who knows absolutely nothing about computers, printing, and publishing, makes it an incredible pleasure to type and write, and they literally do the rest. They are a blessing beyond compare. You would have to work with them to appreciate their near infinite patience and kindness, and their ability to overcome seemingly intractable problems. I am thankful God brought them into my life.

Dan and Ashley Norman have a blessing beyond compare in my life.

My Pastor Paul Mooney is in some ways the greatest man I have ever known. Maybe in all ways. And he is somehow, in a roundabout fashion, responsible for this book. I love you, Pastor.

My companion, my proofreader, and my dear wife Sandi, of course, deserves much credit for this book. Her proofreading prowess is definitely a gift from God.

Any errors or incorrect information are my own. Any benefits from the book are from God, and He deserves the credit. All blessing and honor, and glory belong to Him, world without end, and His innumerable mercies to the sons of men.

Unconditional Eternal Security Is It Scriptural?

What Does the Bible Say About Once Saved Always Saved?

The largest non-Catholic Christian body in the United States is the Southern Baptist Convention, also known as Great Commission Baptists. There are also numerous other Baptist Associations and Conventions. One core tenet that unites almost every Baptist is the doctrine of "Once Saved Always Saved", also known as Unconditional Eternal Security. Is it a Biblical doctrine? Does it promote Godly Christian living? Let me begin with assuring the reader this is definitely not a missive attacking Baptists. I love Baptists and many are extraordinarily sincere and scrupulous in following Holy Writ. However, it is possible to be sincerely wrong. And in love we will examine this doctrine for these precious people. We will attempt to answer the question of the Biblicalness of Unconditional Eternal Security in this brief treatise. Know I come from a long line of Baptists. I have many in my extended family who are of that Faith. I do not come at this question with any malice at all. It is based on love, and the truth of Scripture. While I would have personal doctrinal disagreements with other parts of Baptist doctrine as well, I have felt strongly to teach on this particular question. Some Baptists define as a cult - someone who does not believe in Unconditional Eternal Security. So to them, this is not some minor doctrine, but a core tenet of faith. So let's begin our examination of UES to see if it is Biblical.

Chapter 1

Most feel that Unconditional Eternal Security (UES) has its beginnings as the Fifth of Calvin's Five Points of Calvinism, the Perseverance of the Saints. While many Baptists in the USA are not Five Point Calvinists, most have almost in unison retained this fifth point. But is it Scriptural? Most non-Liturgical people professing Christianity would classify as Bible believers, adherents to Sola Scriptura. Liturgical Christians in many instances would give great credence to traditions of various sorts. So we are interested in the Biblical veracity of UES, not tradition.

There are four undisputable New Testament Passages that seem to spell the death knell for UES. Taken in context, it is really impossible to interpret these New Testament Passages in any other way than one would conclude that UES is unscriptural. I have presented these four Scriptural Passages to adherents in various forums, online and in person, and while some have tried to respond, I have never received an adequate response. Only an intense convoluting of Scripture to maintain this doctrine at all costs was presented to me.

That is not to say that these are the only Scriptures that teach against UES, far from it. Lord willing, we will present many more. But these four foundational Scriptures are really unexplainable in light of UES. The rest will be ancillary Scriptures, building upon this unassailable foundation.

Before we get started, some may ask why would people feel that Scripture teaches UES? That is a valid question. Whether it is presented analogously as once a son always a son, or nothing being able to take us from the Father's Hand, to the power of the Vine in John 15 etc., most arguments I have been presented with are arguments of logic and analogy, not Bible. If UES is not true, then salvation is dependent upon us and not God, many say. Other evidence presented is similar, logic and analogy. If we were to only look at this evidence for UES, then of course, we would find it. Much has to do with our starting point. If we start with the assumption UES is true, then we would tend to bend Scripture to fit that belief. All of us are in danger of doing that on various doctrines. That is the importance of objectivity, going wherever the Scripture leads us. Now the argument could be made that I'm beginning with the starting point of it not being true, so I'll of course fit Scripture to find that narrative. That is why objectivity and a love for Truth is so important. Bias can distort. I have tried to go into this with an open mind. I read books affirming the doctrine of UES. I was raised in a Church that believed it. Yet in my dozens of times through Scripture, I have found more and more evidence that it simply is not true. Let me show you some of that evidence.

Chapter 2

The first Passage we will examine is found in Romans 13, that great submission to earthly government Chapter (With limits. That particular discussion is far beyond the realms of this book. I have multiple Youtube teachings on the subject). It reads:

Verse 1 *"Let every soul be subject unto the higher powers. For there is no power but of God: the powers that be are ordained of God."*

Verse 2 *"Whosoever therefore resisteth the power, resisteth the ordinance of God: and they that resist shall receive to themselves damnation."*

For the sake of examining UES, Verse 2 is most pertinent. It says people who resist the power of lawful government shall receive to themselves damnation. Eternal punishment. Eternal separation from God. This seems rather straight forward. We have to remember that Romans is an Epistle. Epistles are written to saved people, ones who are already Christians. So these people are currently saved, and when they resist the government, they become lost. End of story. Or is it?

The pushback I have received on this, and the other Big Four Passages we are looking at currently, is to immediately go to the lexicons. This is usually the defense of one who does not have an argument. The greatest Biblical linguists of the past 1,400 years made a mistake. Yeah, that's it, they would contend. But proper use of the lexicons, taking the words in context, show there are no mistranslations here. It reads as it is supposed to read.

Next comes an attempt to twist the context of the Passage. But the basics remain. This is written to saved people. Lost people already have damnation on them according to Jesus. They are lost. All of us were at one point and time. Then Jesus saves us. So this is clearly teaching that Christians can lose their salvation. If you go past this Scripture to the Verses beyond, there is no help for this doctrine (UES). Lexicons can't save you. Twisting the context can't help you. Lost people are lost. They are not going to receive to themselves damnation, they are already living in that state. Without salvation, it will become eternal.

So this Passage, plainly and obviously interpreted in context teaches a Christian can lose their salvation. They are currently saved, then they are not. We are not talking about pulling them out of Heaven. But their current state on earth. Let's go to the next one of the Big Four, found also in Romans.

Chapter 3

We have already seen one very obvious Passage that clearly teaches that a person can lose their salvation. Is there another one?

Romans 14:23 reads, "*And he that doubteth is damned if he eat, because he eateth not of faith: for whatsoever is not of faith is sin.*"

The context of this Verse is deciding doubtful things for Christians and how to live in Christian unity. Again, as was Chapter 13, and all of the Epistles, it is written to Christians. And this is very clear from the context. It is speaking of meats. Some feel this has to do with OT dietary laws. Others think that is referring to a group mentioned in early Christian writings that thought Christians when saved went back into an Edenic state. And since they were vegetarians before the Fall, and quite possibly all the way to the Flood, these people would not eat meats. Paul was saying these are minor issues. Everyone should just get along. What day of the week to worship fell in this category as well. What is clear, is that this Passage is to Christians.

And if a Christian has a personal conviction that they should not eat, they are damned if they do eat, violating their conscience. This once again shows eternal punishment to the previously saved. There is no other interpretation. One can go to lexicons and try to twist another translation out of it. But Paul is denoting the serious nature of violating our conscience. If your conscience tells you not to do something, and you do it, you are going to hell. A saved Christian can go to hell. I have done an online Commentary on the Book of Romans in 46 parts which goes into specific detail of the meaning of this Passage. This clearly shows one who is saved, who then becomes damned by violating their conviction, in Paul's Biblical theology.

So we have seen twice, in the great Book of Faith, Romans, that unequivocally you can lose your salvation. But there are yet two other New Testament, post-Pentecost Passages that just as clearly teach the same thing.

Chapter 4

Next we come to teaching on communion. Some say communion is not mentioned in Scripture, when it most certainly is. Others say communion is meant to be spiritual and not actual, when the evidence shows it is to be physically partaken of. But the object of this study is not communion, as fascinating as that is. But is there a place in Paul's teaching about communion in 1 Corinthians 10 and 11 where he mentions about Saints becoming lost? There most certainly is.

I feel I need to mention before going further the use of capitalization with the words Saint(s) and Christian(s). First, not everyone I refer to as a Christian is necessarily a Biblical Christian. I am using it in a broad sense, as someone who comes out of the Christian tradition or faith system, but is not necessarily a full-fledged Biblical Christian. I may occasionally use the term "Saint" in the same manner, but if I do, it will be quite by accident.

Getting back to the issue at hand, let's look at the particular Passage that seems to clearly show a saved person losing their salvation. It is found in 1 Corinthians 11:29, which reads,

"For he that eateth and drinketh unworthily, eateth and drinketh damnation to himself, not discerning the Lord's body."

The teaching of Scripture is clear, that people without Jesus are lost, or are under damnation (or synonymously condemnation) already, such as Romans 5:16 and 18 or John 3:18. So, lost people are well... lost. So this is obviously a saved person at Church, who is not respecting the Lord's Supper (Communion), and they go from a saved state to a lost state. If they are lost, they would already be in an unsaved state. This is clearly talking about a saved person becoming lost. No amount of argument, analogy, or Scripture twisting can change this fact. If a Christian sins, it is possible for them to be lost. I did want us to examine the next Verse in this regard as well. It reads,

Verse 30 *"For this cause many are weak and sickly among you, and many sleep."*

When they partook of Communion in a non-reverential manner, they got weak and sickly in some instances, and many died. This is analogous to Ananias and Sapphira in Acts 5. When they lied to the Holy Ghost, they died. In the Context of Acts 4:34-5:13, it is strongly suggestive, and even assumed by most, that Ananias and Sapphira were saved. They were part of the Church. But they sinned and died. Now did God say they sinned and got a free trip to Heaven? No, of course not. They sinned and died because they were judged. The strong assumption of almost all is they went to hell. God is Judge, however.

In 1 John 5 we read a related Verse. This is, according to my experience, one of the most hated Verses in the Bible, or couple of Verses. It reads,

Verse 16 *"If any man see his brother sin a sin which is not unto death, he shall ask, and he shall give him life for them that sin not unto death. There is a sin unto death: I do not say that he shall pray for it."*

Verse 17 *"All unrighteousmess is sin; and there is a sin not unto death."*

There are certain sins people commit, and they drop dead, like Ananias and Sapphira, and the Corinthians of 1 Corinthians 11:30. So, sin brings death. Not just eternal death, not just spiritual death, but sometimes instantaneous physical death. And Paul explains in 1 Cor. 11:30, sometimes the people do not drop dead. Sometimes it causes them to be weak and sickly. And these people who drop dead at Communion, are getting a free ticket out of all the pain and heartache in this world? As he says in Verse 29 they are eating and drinking damnation unto themselves. This is crystal clear. John in 1 John 5:16, 17 also shares that not all sin leads to instantaneous physical death, but some does. But as Paul points out, those that die go into damnation. They are lost forever.

Next, we come to the most convincing of all the NT Passages that refute once saved always saved. I had a Baptist Pastor friend of mine that we went through each of the aforementioned Verses. He struggled, but cast just enough slivers of doubt in his own mind, that he was not immediately convinced. He wanted to study more, thinking that possibly there was still a way out, especially with lexical aids. When he got to the next Scripture, he immediately went to the lexicons. He was befuddled. They offered no help, not even a scintilla. Context certainly did not help. He was genuinely perplexed. He admitted it certainly seemed to teach you could lose your salvation. To my knowledge, he never found even a slight rebuttal. If he did, he never got back to me about it.

Chapter 5

This Passage is found with Paul talking about how to take care of widows. It is in 1 Timothy 5 Verses 11 and 12. They read,

"But the younger widows refuse: for when they have begun to wax wanton against Christ, they will marry;"

"Having damnation, because they have cast off their first faith."

In Verse 11, and the preceding Verses, it is clear this is speaking of Christian widows. Certain younger widows would begin to wax wanton against Christ. They then marry. They then have damnation because they have cast off their first faith.

Verse 12 not only gives the punishment, it gives the cause. The reason they have damnation, is because they have cast off their first faith. Since only Christianity saves, this faith that is spoken of is obviously speaking of true Christianity. And the punishment is damnation, or one who is consigned, at least at that moment, for hell.

We have gone through how people who are not saved are consigned to hell already. They are going there without salvation. So this Verse, and all of the Big Four Verses we have examined are nonsensical, unless they are talking about saved people who then become lost.

Not only is this obviously talking about a saved person becoming unsaved in this Passage, there is no other interpretation remotely plausible. These Four Passages exist as if God was really trying to emphasize that a true Christian could genuinely lose their salvation based on their sinful actions. Adam lost Eden because of sin. Satan lost heaven because of sin. We lose salvation when we sin. It is that simple. This Passage in 1 Timothy 5 is simply irrefutable. Waxing wanton against Christ. Casting off their first faith. They were definitely saved, then enter a state of damnation. Could they repent? Probably. But they are lost if they don't. Once saved people here, very clearly, become lost.

This Verse stands tall in proclaiming Christians need to live a life of holiness by the help of God. Without God we cannot be holy. But without holiness, no man shall see the Lord. The doctrine of UES leads so often to moral laxity. A little leaven leavens the whole lump. But when we realize that we can go to hell even after we have become saved in this life, we want to be holy, because God is holy (1 Peter 1:15, 16).

Chapter 6

While the preceding four Passages are the clearest and most irrefutable concerning the incorrectness of UES, this is not all the Bible has to say on the subject. We will now go through several Scriptures that continue to teach consistently that a saved person can be lost. Remember, most of the teaching contrary to that is not overtly Biblical and is not consistent with the rest of Scripture. Rather, they are analogies and logic for the most part, and Passages that are looked at in isolation and not with the entirety of the Bible.

As we go through this series of Scriptures, we'll begin in the NT. They won't be in order, per se. We will list the Bible Verse, then give a brief explanation of how it pertains to Unconditional Eternal Security.

Before we get started, I did want to pick some low hanging fruit. Like the fact that Adam and Eve were saved, then booted out of Eden as mentioned in the last Chapter. How Ham was saved through the Flood, and then involved with a terrible episode with his father. The Nation of Israel was saved out of Egypt (Jude 5), and yet none but two made it into the Promised Land over the age of 20.

We begin.

Matthew 5:29, 30 reads,

"And if thy right eye offend thee, pluck it out, and cast it from thee: for it is profitable for thee that one of thy members should perish, and not that thy whole body should be cast into hell."

"And if thy right hand offend thee, cut it off, and cast it from thee: for it

is profitable for thee that one of thy members should perish, and not that thy whole body should be cast into hell."

The context is the Sermon on the Mount. Jesus is speaking of looking on a woman to lust after her. He very clearly teaches you can be saved, then lost by doing this. You go to hell. It is inescapable.

Matthew 7:21 *"Not every one that saith unto me, Lord, Lord, shall enter into the kingdom of heaven; but he that doeth the will of my Father which is in heaven."*

This one is not quite as clear but is given for discussion purposes only. A few of these will fit into this category. It could be teaching that we have to do the will of God after we are saved to enter into the kingdom of heaven. Which means if we don't do it, we don't go to heaven. Now, it could also be saying we have to do God's will to enter into the kingdom of heaven, which is synonymous with the kingdom of God. If that is the case, UES doesn't apply here. But some would say that is very close to works salvation. Again, this is just offered for discussion purposes only. This Verse probably demands more discussion and Context than we have time to give here, so we move on.

Matthew 25:30 *"And cast ye the unprofitable servant into outer darkness: there shall be weeping and gnashing of teeth."*

We see that this servant was given a talent. The servant belonged to the Master, representing Jesus (Verse 14). This servant doesn't increase what he had, and is cast into outer darkness. He was clearly saved, then lost.

Matthew 22:13 *"Then said the king to the servants, Bind him hand and foot, and take him away, and cast him into outer darkness; there shall be weeping and gnashing of teeth."*

Notice that this man makes it to the marriage supper. But he doesn't have a wedding garment on. He was in, but then cast out.

In the parable of the Ten Virgins in Matthew 25, we see that all ten were virgins. They were going to meet Jesus, the Bridegroom. All had lamps. But five were wise and five were foolish. The foolish were then unsaved.

Luke 8:13 *"They on the rock are they, which, when they hear, receive the word with joy; and these have no root, which for a while believe, and in time of temptation fall away."*

This is the second of the four types and conditions of soil, often called the parable of the sower. We see here they believe and have received the word with joy. But in a time of temptation they fall away. They are clearly saved, and just as clearly then lost. Later, we will look at the other types of soil, and how they pertain to UES as well. But these past few Passages are nonsensical if a believer cannot be lost.

Luke 9:62 *"And Jesus said unto him, No man, having put his hand to the plough, and looking back, is fit for the kingdom of God."*

This is a clear instance of someone who puts their hand to the plow, indicating they are saved. They then look back, and are not fit for the kingdom of God. They are lost.

As an aside, Lot's wife was saved out of Sodom. But she looked back and became a pillar of salt. I don't think she was saved because of her disobedience.

John 15:2 *"Every branch in me that beareth not fruit he taketh away: and every branch that beareth fruit, he purgeth it, that it may bring forth more fruit."*

This is very clear. You are in Jesus, which means you are saved (1 Corinthians 12:13). You are a branch. You are of the same kind as the vine. The same sap of the vine flows through you. But if you don't bear fruit, you are removed from the vine. You become unsaved. Verses 4-6 serve to reinforce this point. They read,

"Abide in me, and I in you. As the branch cannot bear fruit of itself, except it abide in the vine; no more can ye, except ye abide in me."

"I am the vine, ye are the branches: He that abideth in me, and I in him, the same bringeth forth much fruit: for without me ye can do nothing."

"If a man abide not in me, he is cast forth as a branch, and is withered; and men gather them, and cast them into the fire, and they are burned."

Verse 6 goes into the process of being taken away by God from the vine. He is cast forth, then becomes withered. They are then burned. Clearly a case of being saved, then becoming lost.

1 Corinthians 9:27 *"But I keep under my body, and bring it into subjection: lest that by any means, when I have preached to others, I myself should be a castaway."*

Without question Paul was saved. If anyone was saved, the great Apostle Paul was. But he said if he didn't keep his body under, he could become a castaway. He without doubt understood that even though he was saved, if he didn't crucify his flesh he could be lost. That is the clear meaning of this Verse.

Next we come to five Verses spoken by Paul that are illustrative of the possibility of falling. 1 Corinthians 10:8-12 says,

"Neither let us commit fornication, as some of them committed, and fell in one day three and twenty thousand."

"Neither let us tempt Christ, as some of them also tempted, and were destroyed of serpents."

"Neither murmur ye, as some of them also murmured, and were destroyed of the destroyer."

"Now all these things happened unto them for ensamples: and they are written for our admonition, upon whom the ends of the world are come."

"Wherefore let him that thinketh he standeth take heed lest he fall."

Notice the verbage here used: fell, destroyed, destroyed (again), fall. And Verse 11 very clearly indicates that these are for our ensamples. If we sin, we too will fall and be destroyed. We see as well how close this is to Chapter 11, and one of the four incontrovertible pillars showing UES is not true. These Verses definitely show you can fall from grace, and be destroyed (lost forever).

Galatians 5:4 reads *"Christ is become of no effect unto you, whosoever of you are justified by the law; ye are fallen from grace."*

This could just as easily be added to one of the four pillars showing

UES is false. The Galatians were clearly saved. It is an Epistle, written to Church people as we rightly divide the word of truth. But Christ, who had saved them, becomes of no effect to them. A process begins of making someone unsaved who was saved. Why? Because they felt the law justified them instead of Jesus. Jesus plus anything makes the Jesus part of none effect. Then Paul gives the coup de grace. They are fallen from grace if they trust in the law for salvation. They were saved. Become is a key word showing that they are leaving their saved state for an unsaved one. And the last phrase, "ye are fallen from grace", shows indisputably they become lost. How much clearer could it be? Don't trust in a false doctrine to sin a little bit every day. Let the power of God deliver you from sin!

Galatians 1:6 says, *"I marvel that ye are so soon removed from him that called you into the grace of Christ unto another gospel:"*
Certainly if one believes a false gospel, they are no longer saved. More evidence that once saved always saved is an incorrect doctrine.

The next four Verses, found in Hebrews 10:26-29, and it could go further into the Chapter, certainly sound irrefutable in reference to UES being invalid. They read thus,
"For if we sin wilfully after that we have received the knowledge of the truth, there remaineth no more sacrifice for sins,"
"But a certain fearful looking for of judgment and fiery indignation, which shall devour the adversaries."
"He that despised Moses' law died without mercy under two or three witnesses:"
"Of how much sorer punishment, suppose ye, shall he be thought worthy, who hath trodden under foot the Son of God, and hath counted the blood of the covenant, wherewith he was sanctified, an unholy thing, and hath done despite unto the Spirit of grace?"
So let's examine this. We sin willfully after we have a knowledge of the truth. This is of course a euphemism for being saved. It really has to be. Notice Paul, or the Writer of Hebrews, says "we". It is clearly talking about the Church in this context, being an Epistle. Next, in Verse 27, he says Church members who willfully sin are looking

fearfully at judgment and indignation, the same judgment that will devour our adversaries. If we sin the way they do, we get the same punishment.

Verses 28 and 29 coalesce with the principle that the New Covenant has higher standards and moral obligations than the Old Covenant. So, if one despised Moses' Law and was killed by the witness of two or three, we should expect a sorer punishment. We have done much worse. He lists three things that make it worse than disobeying Moses' law in the OT. We die lost and go to hell when we sin willfully after we are saved unless we repent. There is no "once saved always saved" taught in Scripture. It is a myth. Jude warned us about people who would turn the grace of God into lasciviousness, when he said in Verse 4 of his Epistle, "For there are certain men crept in unawares, who were before of old ordained to this condemnation, ungodly men, turning the grace of our God into lasciviousness, and denying the only Lord God, and our Lord Jesus Christ."

Paul also brings this out in Romans 6:1 and 2 when he says, "What shall we say then? Shall we continue in sin, that grace may abound?" "God forbid. How shall we, that are dead to sin, live any longer therein?" It is a fearful thing to fall into the hands of the living God. That was written to Church people (Hebrews 10:31).

The Hebrews Passage could be listed among the unassailable Scriptures that disprove UES without a doubt. We now come to another Scriptural Passage that pertains to UES. It is found in Romans 11:20-22. Paul is here discussing under the Inspiration of the Holy Ghost how the Jews lost out, and Gentiles were graffed into the Vine. This is how it reads,

"Well; because of unbelief they were broken off, and thou standest by faith. Be not highminded, but fear:"

"For if God spared not the natural branches, take heed lest he also spare not thee."

"Behold therefore the goodness and severity of God: on them which fell, severity; but toward thee, goodness, if thou continue in his goodness: otherwise thou also shalt be cut off."

The Jews, in mass, but not every Jew of course, because Paul, Silas,

Peter, James, John, etc. were all Jews, but Jews in general were cut off from being exclusively God's people by unbelief. They didn't believe, by and large, when the Messiah came.

But Paul is making a plain case that if Gentiles do not stand by faith, we will be broken off also. Now, some would say this is speaking of groups of people, and not individuals. But what are groups of people made of, except individuals? So, of course, what would go for the group would of necessity go for the individuals within the group, as well.

In Verse 22 he really emphasizes this fact. If we continue, we will be saved. If we do not, we will be cut off. We will be lost. Notice also "thou" is used, which is a singular term. He is speaking to individuals within the groups of Jews and Gentiles he is talking to. So again, we have a clear Passage of Scripture that teaches Unconditional Eternal Security is not true.

I will mention at this point as well. The doctrine of UES, no matter how well intentioned and sincere, usually leads to an erosion of personal holiness. Once you see that you are not once saved always saved, except in eternity of course, you tend to want to please God stronger, knowing your eternal destiny depends on it.

We will deal with one more Passage before we begin a new Chapter. It is found in 2 Peter 2:20-22. It reads,

"For if after they have escaped the pollutions of the world through the knowledge of the Lord and Saviour Jesus Christ, they are again entangled therein, and overcome, the latter end is worse with them than the beginning."

"For it had been better for them not to have known the way of righteousness, than, after they have known it, to turn from the holy commandment delivered unto them."

"But it is happened unto them according to the true proverb, The dog is turned to his own vomit again; and the sow that was washed to her wallowing in the mire."

It is clear that this is speaking of saved people who fall from grace, and get out of right standing with God. In Verse 20, at the beginning, they are saved. They get entangled with the pollutions of the world, are overcome by them, then they are in worse shape than before they were saved. It is impossible to get once saved always saved out of this Passage. How could it be worse without going to hell? Guilt? Shame? Of course none of those things remotely resembles eternal hell fire. But the Passage also indicates the following in Verses 21 and 22, which we will now examine.

Verse 21 reemphasizes the fact they would have been better off not being saved, rather than being saved, then turning back. There are degrees of punishment in hell (Luke 12:47, 48). Verse 22 euphemistically describes them going back to their inward and outward sins. The only correct interpretation of these Verses is that a Christian can turn their back on God and lose their salvation.

Now many try to say how does a forgiven, justified person, become unjustified? The answer is if you break the law after being shown innocent in a Court of Law, you have to answer for the new crime. It is the same way basically in the Heavenly Court of the Universe. We are declared righteous, but He is coming back for a Church without spot, wrinkle, blemish, or any such thing (Ephesians 5:27). There is also the seven times worse principle. If a demon is cast out, if he is allowed to come back, he not only comes back, but brings seven worse than himself (Matthew 12:45), just as the Verses we just read in 2 Peter say. And the people referred to in 2 Peter are definitely not saved. Can they be? Of course, but they need to ask God to forgive them sincerely to get back in right standing with Him.

Chapter 7

The first Verse we will look at here is questionable in regards to UES, but it does serve to show the general principles of God. It refers to Simon the sorcerer in Acts 8:13, and reads,

"Then Simon himself believed also: and when he was baptized, he continued with Philip, and wondered, beholding the miracles and signs which were done."

So, Simon believed and was baptized. Let's compare that to what happened later when he had offered money to know how to lay hands upon people for them to receive the Holy Ghost. Acts 8:20-23 reads thus,

"But Peter said unto him, Thy money perish with thee, because thou hast thought that the gift of God may be purchased with money."

"Thou hast neither part nor lot in this matter: for thy heart is not right in the sight of God."

"Repent therefore of this thy wickedness, and pray God, if perhaps the thought of thine heart may be forgiven thee."

"For I perceive that thou art in the gall of bitterness, and in the bond of iniquity."

So, Simon had believed and been baptized. Now he is pronounced by Peter to: Have neither part nor lot in the matter; his heart was not right with God; He needed to repent of his wickedness and pray; and he was in the gall of bitterness and bond of iniquity.

Verse 21 really surmises the situation well. This believer who had been baptized now has no part or lot in the matter, and his heart was not right with God. There is more we could discuss on this subject, such as the necessity of Spirit baptism, but that is beyond the pale of this short treatise. This really should suffice, and we shall leave it at that.

Next we come to Romans 5:10 which is included simply for discussion purposes. It could be interpreted in a way that would show UES to be false, but it could also be interpreted another way. It reads, *"For if, when we were enemies, we were reconciled to God by the death of his Son, much more, being reconciled, we shall be saved by his life."*

We are reconciled to God by the death of His Son, Jesus. We are saved by His life. Some would say this means the resurrection of Christ, since 1 Corinthians 15 is very clear that the death of Christ without His resurrection is of no benefit to us. Some, however, would interpret this Verse that we are saved by His life living through us. And if this were to cease, we would thence become unsaved. Cease in the sense we disparage the grace of God.

Yet a third interpretation means Christ is ever interceding for us, and that keeps us saved. There may be some indication of that in Romans 8. What is the correct interpretation? In context, it seems that explanation number three may be closest to the context, though good people disagree on the exact meaning. That is the reason I included it here, but under question as it were. It is simply meant for discussion, and really has no bearing ultimately of UES being wrong. A host of other witnesses testify to Unconditional Eternal Security being incorrect!

1 Corinthians 3:17 seems to be a little more straightforward. It says, *"If any man defile the temple of God, him shall God destroy; for the temple of God is holy, which temple ye are."*

In context, it is very clear this is speaking to believers. And God will destroy believers if they defile God's temple. It is speaking of our individual bodies. If we are destroyed, I would assume we are certainly no longer saved. People who are lost are already headed for destruction. "Which temple ye are" seems to clearly be referring to Spirit baptized believers. Just as God's Glory filled the Temple in the Old Testament, now His Spirit indwells New Testament believers. And if we, saved people, defile God's temple, we will be destroyed.

1 John 3:15 has been used by me at times, included in the big four Passages that definitively refute UES. Let's see how. It reads,
"Whosoever hateth his brother is a murderer: and ye know that no murderer hath eternal life abiding in him."
Brother, in context, is plainly speaking of saved persons. Unsaved people are not our brother in a salvic sense. This is an Epistle after all, and Epistles are written to saved people. So, a saved person who hates their brother does not have eternal life dwelling in them, the Spirit of God. They are not saved at that point. I've asked believers in UES if they were still capable of committing murder. To this point, they have all said yes, they could theoretically get to the point they would murder someone. They have a fallen, sinful nature. When I then show them this Verse, that if they murdered someone, they would no longer be saved, they are left with only two choices: Either there is no such doctrine as UES, or a saved person no longer has the capacity to commit murder. They are highly uncomfortable with the second proposition, knowing the depths of sin, and the so-called 13 natures of the heart found in Matthew and Mark. But either saved people can no longer commit murder, or UES is not true. There is no third alternative. So, 1 John 3:15 is definitively a Scripture that causes a conundrum to a proponent of UES, and if they are honest, invalidates UES as a viable doctrine.

In 1 Corinthians 6:9, the context is believers in Corinth suing one another. Paul calls this out as a great evil. He then says in 6:9, *"Know ye not that the unrighteous shall not inherit the kingdom of God? Be not deceived: neither fornicators, nor idolaters, nor adulterers, nor effeminate, nor abusers of themselves with mankind,"*
He is saying in effect that unrighteous people don't go to Heaven, and they are being unrighteous when they sue their brethren. In Verse 11 he reminds them of their New Birth experience, and that they should not be acting in a bad manner. But he is clearly warning

the Corinthian believers that if they act like unbelievers, they will get the same punishment as unbelievers.

1 Corinthians Chapter 5 is one of the most fascinating Chapters in the entire Bible. Horrible fornication is mentioned. A man is sleeping with his mother. Paul says you can kick them out of the Church and turn them over to satan for the destruction of the flesh, that the spirit may be saved in the Day of the Lord Jesus.

But what if the man didn't repent? Wouldn't he still be unsaved? This will segue us into two more related Passages. The first is found in Matthew 18, which seems to at least be related to the subject of 1 Corinthians 5. In Verse 15 of Matthew 18, Jesus begins to show the power and process of Church discipline. He then says, after the process, let the person being disciplined be unto you as a heathen man and a publican (Verse 17). But in Verse 18 He says, "Verily I say unto you, Whatsoever ye shall bind on earth shall be bound in heaven: and whatsoever ye shall loose on earth shall be loosed in heaven." This seems to be continuing with the process of Church discipline. What the Church has done on earth, God honors it as being bound in Heaven. Or once saved, now unsaved. This seems to be somewhat the process Paul is using here in 1 Corinthians 5.

1 Timothy 1:19, 20 shows us people making shipwreck with their faith, and Paul turning them over to satan, just as he advised the Corinthian believers to do with the man in sexual deviancy. It reads,

"Holding faith, and a good conscience; which some having put away concerning faith have made shipwreck:"

"Of whom is Hymenaeus and Alexander; whom I have delivered unto Satan, that they may learn not to blaspheme."

One would assume from reading these Verses that Paul's reasoning was to see these two people saved, because they had once been saved, and now are lost. The power of delivering unto satan is a subject I have dealt with at some length on Youtube. So Hymenaeus and Alexander were saved, made shipwreck of their faith, and Paul turned them over to satan so they will learn not to blaspheme. Could it be any clearer?

Really, one more Passage might be in order to look at along these lines as well. It is found in Philippians the third Chapter. Verses 18, 19 say,

"(For many walk, of whom I have told you often, and now tell you even weeping, that they are the enemies of the cross of Christ:"

"Whose end is destruction, whose God is their belly, and whose glory is in their shame, who mind earthly things.)"

The context seems rather straightforward that he is speaking of once saved individuals in these two Verses. If he is speaking of the always lost, what surprise is it if they do these things? Sinners' sin. But the cause of Paul's weeping is that these brethren who used to be in Truth, now do these ungodly things. And their end is destruction. It is certainly not salvation! They were once saved, and now lost.

So, in conclusion, just as the fornicator in 1 Corinthians 5 was saved, committed sin, then turned over to satan, this same process has been used other times in the New Testament. Paul knew of others who had been saved in his correspondence to Philippi, who became the enemies of the Gospel. They obviously weren't saved. Once saved is not always saved.

1 Corinthians 15:2 says,
"By which also ye are saved, if ye keep in memory what I preached unto you, unless ye have believed in vain."

Paul is here reminding them of the Gospel Message they are saved by. There are two particular items in this Verse that pertain to Once Saved Always Saved. The first is the use of the word "if". This is a predicate, a qualification, if you will. You are saved, but only if you keep in memory what Paul preached. Of course, what is implied, is that if they forget, they are unsaved.

The second item is the last Phrase. This plainly teaches that it is possible to have believed in vain. That you can believe, then be lost. This also is a corollary to the "if" of the preceding phrase. This Verse could have easily been put into the four irrefutable Verses that began our study. I include the first four because of the use of some form of the word "damnation". That is readily and clearly understood to mean eternal punishment. It is a curse word for that reason.

So, once again we see in 1 Corinthians 15:2 clear evidence that UES cannot possibly be Scripturally true.

2 Corinthians 6:1 reads,
"We then, as workers together with him, beseech you also that ye receive not the grace of God in vain."
This Verse would be non-sensical if you could not be lost after once having been saved. Paul and his helpers are here beseeching the Corinthians to have not received the grace of God in vain. Another way of saying that is that you received salvation, only to become lost again. This is the unambiguous teaching of this Scripture. Yet another Biblical testimony that irrefutably teaches that once you are saved you can indeed be lost.

Galatians 4:11
"I am afraid of you, lest I have bestowed upon you labour in vain."
Paul has been confronting the heresy that the Gospel plus the Law and/or circumcision saves. He has declared that to be another Gospel in Galatians 1:6-9. His belief of the Gospel of Jesus Christ being the only means or vehicle of initial salvation was so strong, and his concern for the Church at Galatia so intense, he was fraught with the possibility that he had worked in vain. Vain means "worthless". It doesn't mean that he had worked to see them saved, enduring incredible types of perils, only to see them not reach their best or receive a full reward. Rather, vain would indicate they would be just as lost as they were before he preached to them. Another unequivocal Scripture showing Once Saved Always Saved is not a Biblical Doctrine.

Galatians 5:2 reads,
"Behold, I Paul say unto you, that if ye be circumcised, Christ shall profit you nothing."
Could it be any clearer? He is saying that once they have been saved by the Gospel of Jesus Christ, if they then shed their own blood in circumcision, mistakenly thinking they must do this to be saved, then this is a grievous enough theological error it invalidates

their New Birth experience. They go from being saved, to being lost. Another clear cut case of losing one's salvation.

1 Timothy 4:16
"Take heed unto thyself, and unto the doctrine; continue in them: for in doing this thou shalt both save thyself, and them that hear thee."
Paul is telling this young Minister to have introspection as pertains to Holiness, and make sure he keeps the doctrine pure. If Timothy will do this, he will remain saved, and the people he ministers to will be saved as well, as long as they take heed to Jesus. Timothy of course, was then presently saved. This is an Epistle written to him to help with ministry. He had gifts imparted to him by the Presbytery and Paul's hand. Acts 16 shows clearly he was a believer as well. How will he save himself, if he was already saved? By continuing in the things Paul mentioned. Which means if he did not continue, he would no longer be saved. There is no other interpretation viable.

Hebrews 3:6
"But Christ as a son over his own house; whose house are we, if we hold fast the confidence and the rejoicing of the hope firm unto the end."
This Verse clearly teaches that our being saved is subject to a condition. In this instance, holding fast the confidence and the rejoicing of the hope firm unto the end. "If", as in Amy Carmichael's famous book, is the operative word here. We are God's house if we do this. By implication, we are not God's house if we do not. There is no other interpretation. Our salvation is conditional on our continuance.

We have many more Scriptures yet to go. Let's suppose you are trying to use a lexicon(s) to twist the Passages used here to show that somehow they don't teach what they plainly do teach. Are you saying that your limited knowledge of Hebrew and Greek, and how to properly use lexical aids, is superior to the greatest compilation of Biblical linguists ever known in the King James Translators? It is merely a desperate attempt to try to make the Scriptures say what they clearly do not say. Trust the Word.

Chapter 8

We are merely trying to make the Chapters short and readable. We continue.

James 2:14, 17, 24

"What doth it profit, my brethren, though a man say he hath faith, and have not works? can faith save him?"

"Even so faith, if it hath not works, is dead, being alone."

"Ye see then how that by works a man is justified, and not by faith only."

We are initially saved by faith, that is clear from Scripture. We continue to stay saved by works pleasing to Jesus, that is equally clear in the Bible. Martin Luther called James an Epistle of straw. Luther was evidently incorrect on the New Birth Experience, the initial plan of salvation. So, all he could see were people here trying to work their way into Heaven. You can't do that. God's grace has provided a plan of salvation, Jesus Christ and His death, burial, and resurrection. That, and that alone is how we are saved. But if we don't continue in works pleasing to God, we lose our salvation, and these Verses are as clear about that as other Verses of Scripture we have looked at.

Unconditional Eternal Security did not enter the Christian lexicon through Scripture, but rather through philosophy. Augustine taught some form of it evidently, and John Calvin picked it up. So, faith initially saves us, but working for Jesus by the power of God keeps us saved after that event. We do not get saved to continue in sin. God forbid. Romans 6:15 reads, *"What then? shall we sin, because we are not under the law, but under grace? God forbid."*

James 2:26 says, *"For as the body without the spirit is dead, so faith without works is dead also."*

Faith is likened to the body. Works is likened to the human spirit here. We can initially be saved, but without works we will be lost. The teaching is plain, and once again there is absolutely no other interpretation viable. Doctrine without works is dead.

Romans 2:13 reinforces this. It says, *"(For not the hearers of the law are just before God, but the doers of the law shall be justified."*

Jude 5, 6

"I will therefore put you in remembrance, though ye once knew this, how that the Lord, having saved the people out of the land of Egypt, afterward destroyed them that believed not."

"And the angels which kept not their first estate, but left their own habitation, he hath reserved in everlasting chains under darkness unto the judgment of the great day."

Jude in the so-called Acts of the Apostates is clearly delineating that just as the Old Testament people of God could lose their salvation, so can we. The word "saved" in Verse 5 is not there by accident, but meant to show the correlation between them and us.

God destroyed saved Israelites and angels, why would we be any different? Jude is saying. He is the LORD, He changes not. Again, this is not one possible interpretation among many. But Scripture has afforded us only one meaning that makes any sense.

2 Peter 1:10

"Wherefore the rather, brethren, give diligence to make your calling and election sure: for if ye do these things, ye shall never fall:"

We see once again the operative word is "if". If you do these things you shall never fall. Of course, the laws of English language demand the opposite clause implied, as well. If you don't do these things, you will fall, or else the entire Verse makes no sense. Why would Peter bother to pen these words if falling from grace was not possible?

1 John 2:24

"Let that therefore abide in you, which ye have heard from the beginning.

If that which ye have heard from the beginning shall remain in you, ye also shall continue in the Son, and in the Father."

The determinative word once again is "if". If the truth remains in us, we continue in the Body of Christ. If not, then of course, we don't. It is that simple. Don't allow your mind to be occluded from the plain speech of Scripture. Satan is the father of lies. The entrance of God's Word giveth light, it giveth understanding to the simple.

2 John 9
"Whosoever transgresseth, and abideth not in the doctrine of Christ, hath not God. He that abideth in the doctrine of Christ, he hath both the Father and the Son."

This Verse means one of two things: Either once you have a correct understanding of the doctrine of Christ you can never lose it. But even that would make the Verse non-sensical and superfluous. Or, that you can transgress in the doctrine of Christ and lose your salvation. That is the obvious interpretation. Once saved, not always saved.

Now some may try to say that you can be saved without the Father and the Son. Copious Scriptures show you and I cannot be saved without Jesus. That is basic New Testament teaching.

Jude 12
"These are spots in your feasts of charity, when they feast with you, feeding themselves without fear: clouds they are without water, carried about of winds; trees whose fruit withereth, without fruit, twice dead, plucked up by the roots;"

Clouds without water is very much like the body without the spirit. It is a great analogy, as the Holy Spirit is likened to water in Scripture. They are also trees, saved. Bearing fruit, but it hangs on the limb and dies. They then cease producing fruit. They then become twice dead. They were dead in sins. Become saved. They then die again. Twice dead. They are then plucked up by the roots. There can really be no plainer teaching in Scripture than the clear exposition that this is showing a saved person becoming lost. It is unfortunate saved people become lost, and God doesn't want it to happen. But it does. Just as He doesn't want anyone to die lost, but they do. He has no pleasure in that, according to Scripture.

Jude 24
"Now unto him that is able to keep you from falling, and to present you faultless before the presence of his glory with exceeding joy,"

It says He is able to keep you from falling, it does not say He will keep you from ever falling. Nothing external can take you out of the Father's hand. But you can willfully leave. It is your choice.

The Epistles found in the introductory part of the Book of Revelation shine light on Christians' ability to fall from grace. These seven Letters to the seven Churches have been so spiritualized, dispensationalized, and allegorized, people many times forget these were seven actual Churches dealing with situations and obtaining promises, etc. Let's examine the pertinent Passages on the subject of UES.

Revelation 2:5 *"Remember therefore from whence thou art fallen, and repent, and do the first works; or else I will come unto thee quickly, and will remove thy candlestick out of his place, except thou repent."*

In Revelation 1:20 we see that the candlestick represents the Church, the seven golden candlesticks representing the seven Churches of Asia, specifically. Here we see that unless the angel repents, probably representing the spiritual leader of the Church, God will come quickly and remove the candlestick. This sounds like the Church will no longer exist. In this context the Church represents the saved people in the Church, so it certainly sounds like the Church will lose their salvation, so to speak.

Even Jesus' Parable of the soils shows us this. One type of soil never gives birth to the seed. The next type germinates the seed, gives birth to a plant. But since it has no deepness of earth, it is offended, or otherwise removed. It loses its salvation. The next grows, but weeds grow up and choke out its life. It brings forth no fruit, and Jesus is very clear a non-fruit bearing tree is cut off and burned. This Parable very definitely teaches one can lose their salvation, just as the Church of Ephesus could have their candlestick removed. They would cease to exist because they did not repent.

Revelation 2:10

"Fear none of those things which thou shalt suffer: behold, the devil shall cast some of you into prison, that ye may be tried; and ye shall have tribulation ten days: be thou faithful unto death, and I will give thee a crown of life."

This Verse is very straightforward. If you are faithful unto death, God will give a crown of life. The specific implication is, if they are not faithful unto death, they will not get a crown of life. Some would argue they would still be saved, just not receive the crown of life. But think about the title of the crown. Of life. Saved Christians will live again in the resurrection. It strongly appears this is speaking of eternal life. So the reciprocal would be you would not receive the crown of life if you're not faithful unto death.

Revelation 2:13

"I know thy works, and where thou dwellest, even where Satan's seat is: and thou holdest fast my name, and hast not denied my faith, even in those days wherein Antipas was my faithful martyr, who was slain among you, where Satan dwelleth."

The angel had not denied God's faith. But the implication is clear. He could have. And of course, we are not saved if we deny the faith. Jesus will in like manner deny us (Matthew 10:33; 2 Timothy 2:13).

Revelation 3:5

"He that overcometh, the same shall be clothed in white raiment; and I will not blot out his name out of the book of life, but I will confess his name before my Father, and before his angels."

This Verse shows us that when Jesus does not confess us before the Father, our names are blotted out of the book of life. The book of life is mentioned eight times in Scripture, and is always dealing with salvation. So plainly, we can be saved, have our names in the book of life, put there when we are saved, then have them removed through sin. Blotted out.

God really reinforces this fact in no uncertain terms in Exodus 32:33, which reads, *"And the LORD said unto Moses, Whosoever hath sinned against me, him will I blot out of my book."* This Verse alone seems to show incontrovertibly that UES is not true, that God can and will blot our names out of the book of life if we sin.

Next we come to Revelation 3:16 and the Church in Laodecia. It says,
"So then because thou art lukewarm, and neither cold nor hot, I will spue thee out of my mouth."
Becoming spittle for Jesus doesn't seem to be a pathway for salvation. We are in Jesus, then we are not part of Jesus, as this Verse tells us.

Revelation 3:21
"To him that overcometh will I grant to sit with me in my throne, even as I also overcame, and am set down with my Father in his throne."
The implicative part of this Verse is clear. If we don't overcome, we won't sit with Jesus on the Throne. In Revelation 21:7, 8 we see the contrast of those who overcome with the lost. There are only two states of mankind, overcomers and the lost. So it is clear if we don't overcome, we will once again become lost.

Revelation 22:19
"And if any man shall take away from the words of the book of this prophecy, God shall take away his part out of the book of life, and out of the holy city, and from the things which are written in this book."
Moving past Chapters 2-3 of Revelation, we come to this Passage. Could it be clearer? People who remove parts of Scripture, saved people, then become lost. Their part is taken out of the book of life, they no longer are part of the New Jerusalem. Scripture could not be more certain that a saved person can indeed become lost.

John 15:10
"If ye keep my commandments, ye shall abide in my love; even as I have kept my Father's commandments, and abide in his love."
The Scripture could not be any more plain. If we don't keep the Father's commandments, we no longer abide in His love. The wrath of God abides in us. This Verse is clearly speaking of a saved person,

who if they keep Jesus' commandments, remain saved. But if not they are lost. Plain as day.

Chapter 9

Several more New Testament, post-Pentecost Scriptures will be presented for your perusal on this subject. The Day of Pentecost is almost universally accepted as the Birthday of the Church, so the Scriptures will be applicable to us. We begin with 1 Corinthians 8:11, which reads,

"And through thy knowledge shall the weak brother perish, for whom Christ died?"

This Passage correlates with Romans 14:23. They are speaking of the same subject. Romans 14:23 reads, *"And he that doubteth is damned if he eat, because he eateth not of faith: for whatsoever is not of faith is sin."*

We see that Paul uses the term "perish" in I Corinthians, and "damned" in Romans, but they are speaking of the same situation. Some could still try to argue the point that the person dies by overriding their conscience, but they are still saved. That is obviously erroneous on two levels. First, the congruent Passage makes it clear that "perish" is synonymous with "damnation". Second, when God strikes someone down with death, is it really to save them? Wouldn't He rather allow them to live since He doesn't rejoice at the death of the wicked? He would give them time to repent (2 Corinthians 7:10; Ezekiel 33:11; 2 Peter 3:9). So there is no once saved always saved.

Speaking of 2 Corinthians 7:10, let's examine it.

"For godly sorrow worketh repentance to salvation not to be repented of: but the sorrow of the world worketh death."

In context, this is speaking of the man who was put out of the Church in 1 Corinthians 5, who later repented and came back in. Paul is also making a broader point to the entire Church at Corinth, as well. Notice it is to the Church, saved people, and not the world. The world is under condemnation already. He says to the Church that godly sorrow worketh repentance to salvation. It means the Church member can lose their salvation. But when they feel badly for their sin, they can repent, and be saved once again. Unconditional Eternal Security is absolutely wrong.

Some people shorten UES to Eternal Security. These are two different things. The Christian has eternal security. Nothing can move you and I from the Father's love (John 10; Romans 8). The Christian can be secure in knowing that while they are following God, no fusillade of satan and his demons can remove you. No circumstance can get you to curse God and die. Sometimes we just have to stand as Ephesians 6 instructs us. The error is in the word "unconditional". That we are saved regardless of our actions. This is plainly not taught in Scripture.

Galatians 5:2

"Behold, I Paul say unto you, that if ye be circumcised, Christ shall profit you nothing."

We mentioned this earlier, but I thought it would be good to focus on it some more. Paul is saying to the saved people of Galatia, that if they think they are not saved until they are circumcised, that Acts 2:38 plus circumcision is a false Gospel. This is such a powerful point. "Christ shall profit you nothing" means you go from a saved state, believing and obeying the Gospel, unto an unsaved state. They are saved, then think they need to be circumcised, as well. Instead of saving them, it un-saves them. This is plainly taught here. Later in this same Chapter, we find another plain instance of believers being able to lose their salvation.

Galatians 5:21

"Envyings, murders, drunkenness, revellings, and such like: of the which I tell you before, as I have also told you in time past, that they which do such things shall not inherit the kingdom of God."

Paul is here listing the 17 or 18 works of the flesh (depending on your count). As he finishes listing them, he reminds the believers if they do these things, they will not be saved. They are acting like unbelievers, they will go to the same eternal destination with unbelievers. This is congruent with Paul's admonition in 1 Corinthians 6:11, examined earlier. If believers sin like unbelievers, we go to hell like they do.

Hebrews 10:38

"Now the just shall live by faith: but if any man draw back, my soul shall have no pleasure in him."

If those that draw back have no pleasure from God, I don't see how they will be saved in the final end. Many people think that this is talking about apostasy. Not just sinning, but repudiating the Gospel, or major portions of the Biblical Faith. That is really a moot point for this study. They are still admitting that a once saved person can be lost. They are saying it is only by apostasy, but they are admitting that Unconditional Eternal Security is incorrect. I have been confronted with this reasoning before, but I have never heard an adequate explanation on how one can believe that once saved always saved is true, yet on the subject of apostasy it is not.

Occasionally one will bring up the point that someone is really not saved until they make Heaven. So they are Once Saved Always Saved. Anyone who studies Scripture knows that salvation has a three-fold aspect. People were saved, are saved, and are going to be saved (for eternity). All three uses are found in Scripture. Of course, once people get to Heaven, they can no longer be lost. This is taught in Scripture. Be we are not in Heaven yet, so that point is moot as well. Some of the other subjects in this paragraph and the preceding are the subject of other studies. But someone who is currently, Biblically saved, can in fact be lost, as seen in this Verse, and the other copious amounts of Scripture looked at to this point.

James 5:19, 20

"Brethren, if any of you do err from the truth, and one convert him;"

"Let him know, that he which converteth the sinner from the error of his way shall save a soul from death, and shall hide a multitude of sins."

In Verse 19, the operative word for our study is "you". This is clearly speaking of saved people, since this is who Epistles are written to. That is Bible Study 101, rightly dividing the Word of Truth. The context here demands that to be the case also. So, this is written to saved people. All who were once saved, and are now unsaved have obviously erred from the truth.

Verse 20 calls this formerly saved person a sinner. He is in error. And he shall die. Now, some say this has to do with the chastening of the LORD. God kills them, but they are saved. That has already been dealt with in some detail with Ananias and Sapphira, the Corinthian Church, and 1 John 5. It is difficult to see how someone is sinning so much that God kills them so they can get a free trip to Heaven. It is almost absurd on its face. The most natural explanation is that we are dealing with a saved person who has erred from the truth, and someone brings him back to Truth. It is good to know that people who go into false doctrine can be saved! But if they don't repent, they will be lost, having once enjoyed salvation.

One other point is the use of the word "soul" in Verse 20. They are not just physically dropping dead. Their soul dies. They are unsaved. This should be clear from the context. UES is here to be seen as untrue.

1 John 2:28

"And now, little children, abide in him; that, when he shall appear, we may have confidence, and not be ashamed before him at his coming."

The implication here is clear. If we don't abide in Him, we become like the branch in John 15. We will be lost.

1 John 2:24

"Let that therefore abide in you, which ye have heard from the beginning. If that which ye have heard from the beginning shall remain in you, ye also shall continue in the Son, and in the Father."

Again, the implication could not be clearer. If that which we have heard from the beginning does not remain in us, we do not continue in the Father and the Son. Other Scriptures looked at in this study have shown this means one is not saved. That is obvious.

The operative word is "if". It does not read in language of finality, but of choice. There is a possibility both ways. You can chose to be saved, or to be lost. Also, the very beginning word "Let" indicates a choice, not a finality. Clearly and plainly this Passage teaches a currently saved person can be lost depending on their actions. This has nothing to do with works salvation. On the contrary, it has to do with salvation coming only by and through Jesus, and after that point showing we love Him keeping His Commandments by the transformative power of the New Birth.

1 John 3:24
"And he that keepeth his commandments dwelleth in him, and he in him. And hereby we know that he abideth in us, by the Spirit which he hath given us."

If we do not keep His commandments, we do not dwell in Him. Now this could mean that everyone who is saved automatically keeps the commandments of God. Some Calvinists actually argue that point, and struggle with who is really saved or not. But that is a monumental stretch, and almost no one would argue that point. We keep His commandments, we are saved. Of course, if we do not, we are lost. No once saved always saved can be construed out of this Verse.

This Verse also teaches a believer can lose the Holy Ghost after salvation. This is irrefutable.

Chapter 10

Philippians 2:12
"*Wherefore, my beloved, as ye have always obeyed, not as in my presence only, but now much more in my absence, work out your own salvation with fear and trembling.*"

This means in a certain, eternal sense, we are not yet saved. We are to choose our actions with fear and trembling. If we don't, the implication is we will be lost.

1 Thessalonians 3:5
"*For this cause, when I could no longer forbear, I sent to know your faith, lest by some means the tempter have tempted you, and our labour be in vain.*"

This is one of the more straightforward Passages showing you can lose your salvation. If the believers in Thessalonica would still spend eternity with Jesus, being like Him, but only lose rewards, Paul's labour would definitely not be in vain. Satan can tempt us and we can make poor decisions, which lead to hell, even after we are saved. It is crystal clear.

Hebrews 3:14
"*For we are made partakers of Christ, if we hold the beginning of our confidence stedfast unto the end;*"

"If" is once again the key word. "If" is a dependent word. We are partakers of Christ, but only if we hold the beginning of our confidence stedfast unto the end. If we don't, we are lost.

Hebrews 8:9

"Not according to the covenant that I made with their fathers in the day when I took them by the hand to lead them out of the land of Egypt; because they continued not in my covenant, and I regarded them not, saith the Lord."

God is the LORD, He changes not (Malachi 3:6). This is known as the immutability and unchangeability of God. If the OT saints were not regarded by God because they didn't continue in the covenant, how much more us? We are constantly reminded of the higher standards of the New Covenant, with sorer punishment for disobedience. UES is once again to be shown impossible Biblically.

Hebrews 12:15, 17

"Looking diligently lest any man fail of the grace of God; lest any root of bitterness springing up trouble you, and thereby many be defiled;"

"For ye know how that afterward, when he would have inherited the blessing, he was rejected: for he found no place of repentance, though he sought it carefully with tears."

In Verse 15, we see we can fail of the grace of God. In Verse 16, not listed here, we see a root of bitterness can spring up causing one to be a fornicator, which 1 Corinthians 6 clearly states doesn't inherit the kingdom of God.

Verse 17 says he was rejected. He no longer had the inheritance or the blessing (Esau). That is an ensample to us according to Scripture.

Joshua 7:12

"Therefore the children of Israel could not stand before their enemies, but turned their backs before their enemies, because they were accursed: neither will I be with you any more, except ye destroy the accursed from among you."

Almost all of the examples to this point have been from the New Testament. But since God does not change, a few examples from the OT will suffice. Here we have Achan taking the accursed thing. He confesses, yet dies without mercy. He was accursed. The implications for salvation seem clear.

Leviticus 18:29

"For whosoever shall commit any of these abominations, even the souls that commit them shall be cut off from among their people."

We find an interesting phenomenon in the Law. A person who violates certain aspects of the Law becomes cut off. One of the arguments in favor of UES is that once an Israelite, always an Israelite. You couldn't unbecome being Jewish. But as we will repeatedly see, as in the Verse, the Israelite souls who commit abominations are cut off. This doesn't just mean they're put out of the Tribe. To be saved, they had to go through Feasts such as Passover, Trumpets, and Yom Kippur every year. So, when they were cut off, they were cut off from the promises and blessings of God. They were, evidently, and the evidence is overwhelming to this, unsaved. You can be disinherited from the family.

Leviticus 19:8

"Therefore every one that eateth it shall bear his iniquity, because he hath profaned the hallowed thing of the LORD: and that soul shall be cut off from among his people."

Notice once again a Hebrew who disobeys shall bear his iniquity, and the soul shall be cut off from among his people. It is the soul, not just the physical body for chastening from the LORD.

Leviticus 22:3

"Say unto them, Whosoever he be of all your seed among your generations, that goeth unto the holy things, which the children of Israel hallow unto the LORD, having his uncleanness upon him, that soul shall be cut off from my presence: I am the LORD."

Notice a distinctive feature of this Verse is that the soul will be cut off from God's Presence, not just His people. This seems to definitively show that the person is no longer part of the people and promises of God. The use of the word "soul", instead of "individual" or something similar, is instructive, as well.

Ezekiel 18:24

"But when the righteous turneth away from his righteousness, and

committeth iniquity, and doeth according to all the abominations that the wicked man doeth, shall he live? All his righteousness that he hath done shall not be mentioned: in his trespass that he hath trespassed, and in his sin that he hath sinned, in them shall he die."

A righteous man that turns to sin shall die. His righteousness that he has done will not be mentioned. He is lost. Really, the entire 18th Chapter of Ezekiel could be exegeted to show the fact that saved people can sin, then be lost.

1 Samuel 2:30

"Wherefore the LORD God of Israel saith, I said indeed that thy house, and the house of thy father, should walk before me for ever: but now the LORD saith, Be it far from me; for them that honour me I will honour, and they that despise me shall be lightly esteemed."

Notice the wording: Eli's house was to walk before Jehovah Elohim for ever. But now it is far from God. Once saved, not always saved, in other words.

Leviticus 23:29, 30

"For whatsoever soul it be that shall not be afflicted in that same day, he shall be cut off from among his people."

"And whatsoever soul it be that doeth any work in that same day, the same soul will I destroy from among his people."

This is concerning the Day of Atonement. A soul that doesn't fast (be afflicted) on that day will be cut off from among his people. Does this mean they will drop dead? Spiritually, at least.

If someone works on the Day of Atonement, Yom Kippur, God will destroy them from among his people. It certainly doesn't sound like He will save them for eternity. If so, what is the point for the judgement?

Conclusion

We began our study with four indisputable Scriptures, that taken contextually, refute Unconditional Eternal Security. We then began to examine dozens of other Passages, that to mostly greater, but some lesser degrees, also make belief in Unconditional Eternal Security incompatible with Scripture.

Such analogies and logic, as once a son always a son, nothing, not even us, are able to remove us from the Father's Hand, etc. are able to rebut the clear teaching of Scripture from the Garden of Eden to the Book of Revelation. Mankind, once saved, if he acts according to sin, will be lost. The evidence is conclusive.

The Holiness Movement of the 1800's was born primarily of people who believed you could lose your salvation. This motivated them to live for God, so they could make Heaven. Once UES took over vast swaths of American Christianity, a detrimental let down of personal holiness was the result.

Believe the Bible. Adhere to Scripture. Obey Acts 2:38, and then be holy as He is holy. This is the plan and pathway to Bible Salvation. Enoch means "dedicated". He was raptured because he walked with God. If you love Jesus, keep His commandments. May God richly bless you as you walk with Him.

Other Books by Steven Waldron

Commentary On Genesis Volume 1
Discussions In Scripture Series
A Creationist Commentary

Commentary On Genesis Volume 2
Discussions In Scripture Series
A Creationist Commentary

Commentary On Genesis Volume 3
Discussions In Scripture Series
A Creationist Commentary

www.ingramcontent.com/pod-product-compliance
Lightning Source LLC
Chambersburg PA
CBHW030202100526
44592CB00009B/403